CARTOONS OF COERCION
TYRANNY OF KING GEORGE III RESTORED
BUT UNDER NEW MANAGEMENT

BY FELTON WILLIAMSON, JR.

ISBN-13: 978-1495266065

ISBN-10: 1495266060

HOW TO GET THE MOST FROM THIS BOOK

Publishing a book with illustrations for the Kindle format is complicated. Unfortunately, the actual Kindle display varies from device to device and so does the page length. The Kindle platform must present its image on displays from 4 inches wide to the width of your computer screen. The formatting of the manuscript must be compromised to present acceptable images on all platforms. To provide the largest display on smaller screens and minimize blank pages, this book was formatted so that the image (cartoon) fills the full page. On most platforms, the caption for the image will be displayed, alone, on the page before the image. Early Kindles (before the Kindle Paper White platform) will have a blank page between the caption and the image. Generally, the caption will be displayed alone on the page. Apologies for the blank pages on the older Kindles but it is the best compromise, eliminating the blank pages causing problems on all the other platforms.

The Table of Contents will contain the captions for all of the images. By going to the Table of Contents and clicking on the caption, the page with the caption will be displayed. When you advance to the next page, the image will be displayed, thus allowing you to easily display an image on your portable device, such as the Kindles, iPhone, iPAD, computer or Android. This format makes it easy to display a particular cartoon to a friend using your portable device.

Care should be taken when displaying these cartoons to friends and acquaintances. Some of these cartoons may invoke violent behavior or even medical emergencies when displayed to the Aristocracy and their cronies. The same reaction may occur when displaying the cartoons to persons with impaired logic (often referred to as Liberals) who believe that the use of government force can lead to a better life.

Software to read the Kindle editions on your computer is available from Amazon.com at no cost. If you enjoy the cartoons in this book and want the best presentation of those images, I suggest that you download the Kindle software for your computer from Amazon. Go to the following link:
http://www.amazon.com/gp/feature.html/ref=sv_kstore_3?ie=UTF8&docId=1 000493771

This book provides minimal background on the conditions that led to the creation of these cartoons. If you wish more background information on these cartoons, the book "21st Century Common Sense" also by Felton Williamson, Jr. will provide that information at minimal cost.

You are certain to find many cartoons that you want to discuss your friends and acquaintances. It's easy to begin an interesting conversation with the display of these controversial cartoons.

INTRODUCTION

The United States Constitution is not a perfect document, but it was the best effort of the Founding Fathers based on the knowledge, customs and traditions of 1787. For over 100 years, the Constitution provided a level of prosperity and well-being that was unique in the history of the world. The flaws in the Constitution allowed those who consider themselves the Aristocracy with exceptional rights to corrupt the Constitution and usurp those rights. With promises of unearned wealth and security to the masses, the Aristocracy obtained support for the corruption of the Constitution. Thus, the Aristocracy has accumulated the power and wealth they felt was their due.

In the beginning, the Aristocracy's progress of corrupting the Constitution was very slow. Immediately upon the ratification of the Constitution, the counter-revolution began. But the Aristocracy made very little progress until 1888. In 1888, the Bureaucracy was established by the creation of the Interstate Commerce Commission (ICC). The mechanism for the use of the government's monopoly on force for the benefit of the politically powerful was established and in place. It's been downhill ever since!

"*CARTOONS OF COERCION*" is composed of cartoons exposing the Aristocracy's violence to the Constitution. Amending the Constitution by reinterpretation has empowered the Aristocracy and stripped the masses of the rights guaranteed to them by the Constitution. This is what the Aristocracy means when they speak of a "living breathing Constitution." This Aristocracy has achieved tremendous power and wealth and has almost reinstated the tyranny of King George III, under their management. A free and prosperous people are being converted into 21st Century serfs.

Periodically, short sections of text will be included to explain the purpose and conditions that led to the creation of the cartoons. Each of the illustrations is listed in the Table of Contents and may be accessed by clicking on the title of the illustration. The purpose of this format is to allow the reader to easily use the Kindle, iPod or other device to present these illustrations to friends. The reader is cautioned to be very selective in presenting these illustrations to the disciples of the Elite as it may provoke hostility or inflame an existing medical emergency condition.

To remove any question of semantics, the term Aristocracy and Elite is used to describe those who seek to use the government's monopoly on force to accrue personal wealth and power.

Remember, the contents of this book are primarily cartoons. The creator of cartoons has a poetic license to display exaggerated circumstances to prove the point. A certain amount of exaggeration is necessary to produce interesting and outrageous cartoons.

This "Table of Contents" lists all illustrations and some text passages. The reader may go to any subject or cartoon by clicking on the title. On Kindle devices this "Table of Contents" will be several pages in length; the number of pages depends on the display size of the device. There will be a statement marking the end of the "Table of Contents."

Table of Contents

END OF TABLE OF CONTENTS

ECONOMIC SYSTEMS

"Wikipedia Encyclopedia" lists 52 different economic systems. Actually, there are only three different classes of economic systems. These are the "TYRANNY", the "MIXED ECONOMY" (cronyism) and "CAPITALISM". There is little to be gained by rigorously defining a "MIXED ECONOMY" economic system as they change every time the legislature meets and a new group of cronies come to power.

The TYRANNY ECONOMIC SYSTEM is total control of the economy by a dictator or very small counsel. It is characterized by confiscation of wealth and punishing of dissent. Political dissent is not tolerated. The Aristocracy justifies the theft and coercion by the claim that they are acting for the common good. TYRANNY ECONOMIC SYSTEM goes by many names, Communism, Socialism, Fascism, Dictatorship, Kings, Emperors, Sheiks, Tribal Chief – Witch Doctor and other concocted names that attempt to hide the true nature of the Dictator.

The "CAPITALISM (FREE ENTERPRISE) ECONOMIC SYSTEM" is individual freedom; the government protects the individual from the initiation of physical force and violence, both foreign and domestic. The pure Capitalistic Economic System has never existed. Like the temperature "absolute zero" in physics, it has only been approached. Perhaps the closest thing to a Capitalistic Economic System existed in the United States for a period of time after the Constitution was ratified. The definition of the Capitalist Economic System sounds simple but that is deceptive. For instance, to protect the individual from the initiation of force and violence, it is both cost-effective and humanitarian to provide a destitute individual with minimal subsistence than to incarcerate them when hunger forces violent behavior. For more on the definition of pure Capitalism, research the writings of Ayn Rand or "21st Century Common Sense".

The "Mixed Economy Economic System" is simply a mixture of freedom and tyranny. It changes with each session of the legislature and the objectives of the political cronies controlling the politicians. As the oppression of the individual slowly grows, the economic conditions worsen. The Aristocracy uses the decaying economic conditions to justify more oppression of the individual. The increased oppression enhances the Aristocracy's wealth and power. The trend is certainly toward the extreme Left, the Totalitarian Economic System.

GRAPH - FREEDOM V/S PROSPERITY

Throughout history, those civilizations that have enjoyed the most individual freedom have also been the most prosperous. That fact is illustrated in this graph.

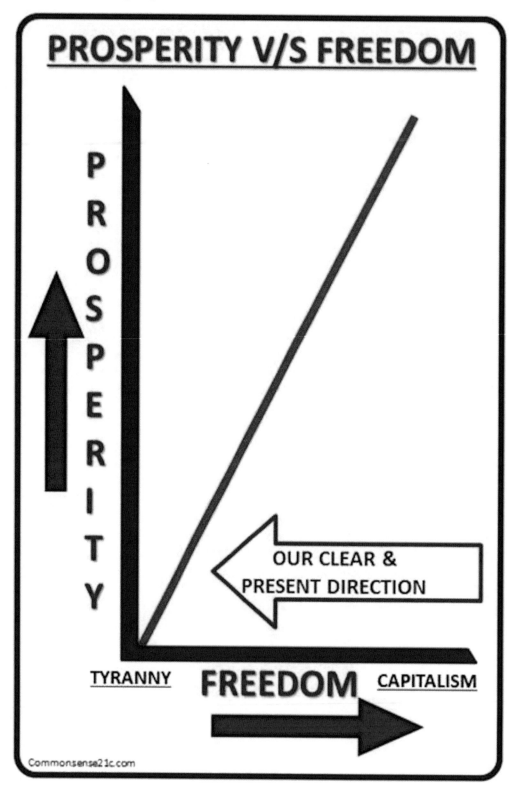

The cartoon displays the economic consequences of Tyranny and the coercion by the Aristocracy. Our Mixed Economy Economic System is rapidly moving to the extreme left. If this trend continues, we will become the 21st Century serfs.

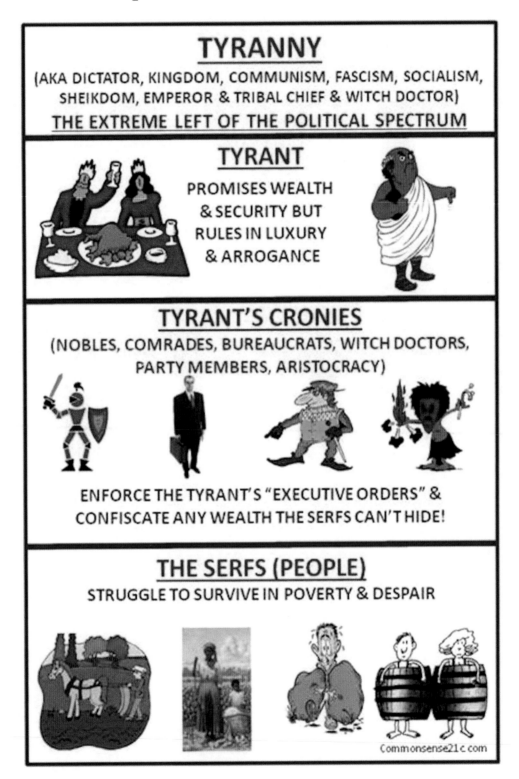

PERFORMANCE OF THE MIXED ECONOMY SYSTEM

The disastrous consequences of the Mixed Economy Economic System are displayed. The change from the Mixed Economic System to Tyranny is accelerating. Increasing coercion is driving us into poverty and despair.

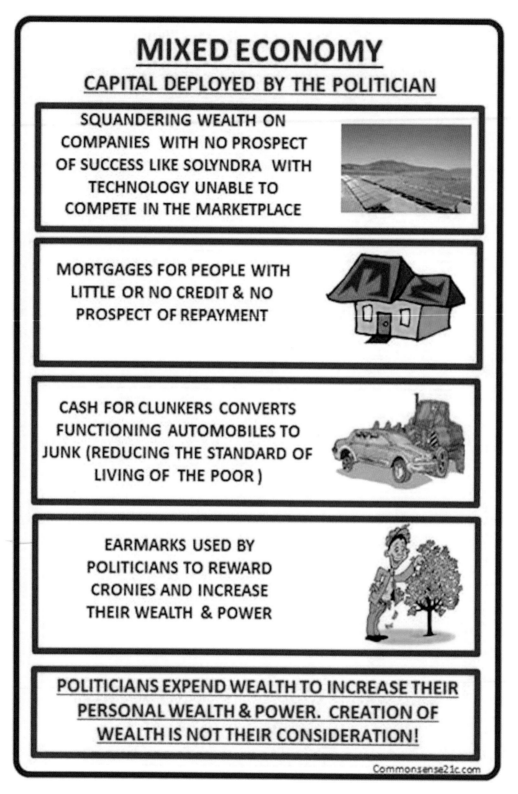

CAPITALISM PERFORMANCE

This cartoon displays some of the early accomplishments 18th & 19th Century Capitalism. Tremendous wealth was created before Aristocracy accumulated its power. Pure Capitalism has never existed. It is interesting to speculate on what might have been accomplished if our earlier government had been closer to Capitalism.

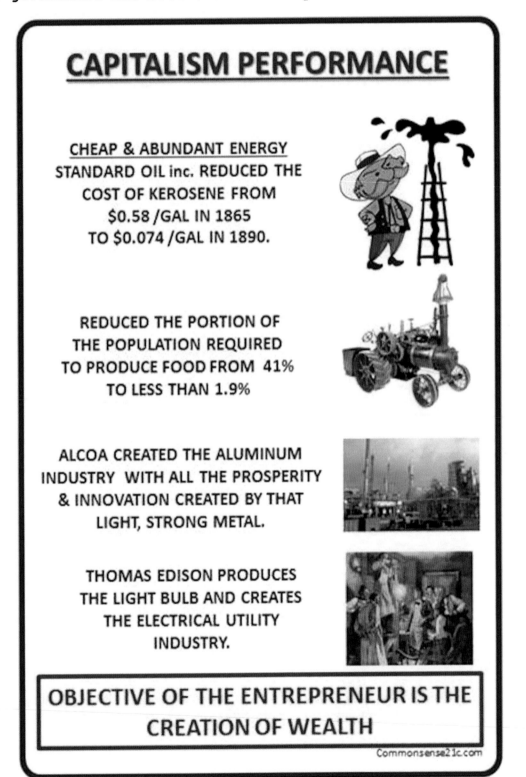

CAPITALISM PERFORMANCE

CHEAP & ABUNDANT ENERGY
STANDARD OIL inc. REDUCED THE
COST OF KEROSENE FROM
$0.58 /GAL IN 1865
TO $0.074 /GAL IN 1890.

REDUCED THE PORTION OF
THE POPULATION REQUIRED
TO PRODUCE FOOD FROM 41%
TO LESS THAN 1.9%

ALCOA CREATED THE ALUMINUM
INDUSTRY WITH ALL THE PROSPERITY
& INNOVATION CREATED BY THAT
LIGHT, STRONG METAL.

THOMAS EDISON PRODUCES
THE LIGHT BULB AND CREATES
THE ELECTRICAL UTILITY
INDUSTRY.

OBJECTIVE OF THE ENTREPRENEUR IS THE CREATION OF WEALTH

Commonsense21c.com

The results of Capitalism & Tyranny compared.

USE OF CAPITAL

The difference between the economic systems is the purpose of deploying capital. The entrepreneur deploys capital to create wealth and earn a profit. The politician uses capital (money) to maintain and increase his power.

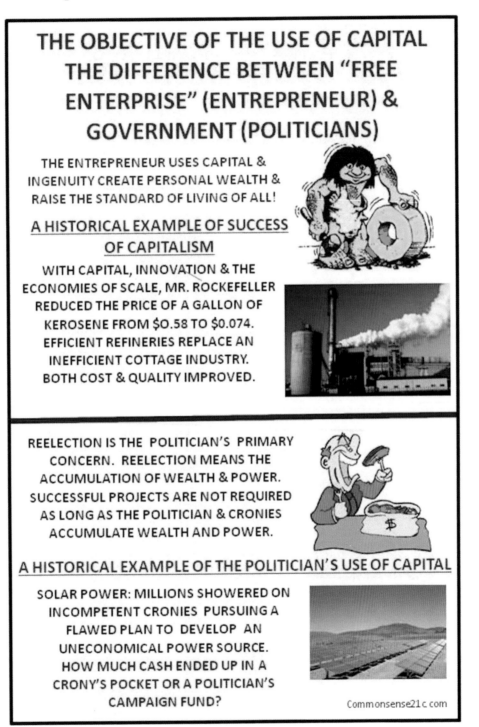

THE OBJECTIVE OF THE USE OF CAPITAL
THE DIFFERENCE BETWEEN "FREE ENTERPRISE" (ENTREPRENEUR) & GOVERNMENT (POLITICIANS)

THE ENTREPRENEUR USES CAPITAL & INGENUITY CREATE PERSONAL WEALTH & RAISE THE STANDARD OF LIVING OF ALL!

A HISTORICAL EXAMPLE OF SUCCESS OF CAPITALISM

WITH CAPITAL, INNOVATION & THE ECONOMIES OF SCALE, MR. ROCKEFELLER REDUCED THE PRICE OF A GALLON OF KEROSENE FROM $0.58 TO $0.074. EFFICIENT REFINERIES REPLACE AN INEFFICIENT COTTAGE INDUSTRY. BOTH COST & QUALITY IMPROVED.

REELECTION IS THE POLITICIAN'S PRIMARY CONCERN. REELECTION MEANS THE ACCUMULATION OF WEALTH & POWER. SUCCESSFUL PROJECTS ARE NOT REQUIRED AS LONG AS THE POLITICIAN & CRONIES ACCUMULATE WEALTH AND POWER.

A HISTORICAL EXAMPLE OF THE POLITICIAN'S USE OF CAPITAL

SOLAR POWER: MILLIONS SHOWERED ON INCOMPETENT CRONIES PURSUING A FLAWED PLAN TO DEVELOP AN UNECONOMICAL POWER SOURCE. HOW MUCH CASH ENDED UP IN A CRONY'S POCKET OR A POLITICIAN'S CAMPAIGN FUND?

Commonsense21c.com

CAPITALISM OR CRONYISM

Life under the Capitalist Economic System is compared to life under the Cronyism Economic Systems.

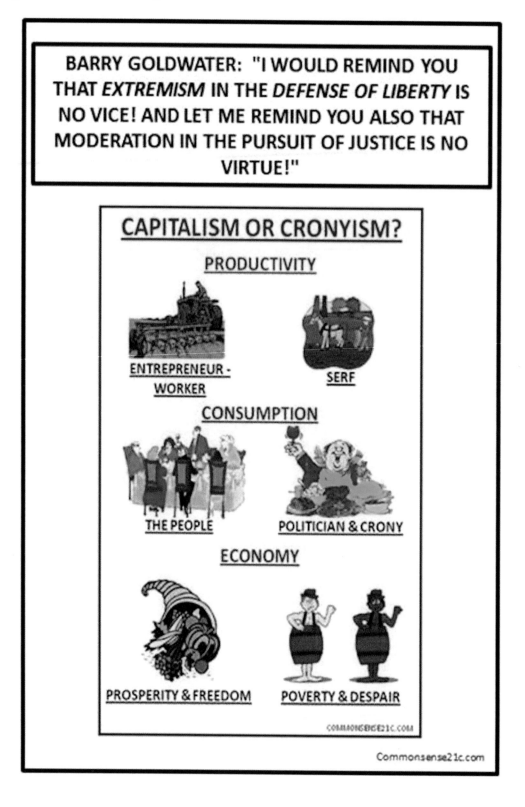

The forces of Tyranny, now, in 1776 and in prehistoric times

WEALTH MUST BE PRODUCED BEFORE CONSUMED

Wealth is the food, shelter, transportation, services and means of production that are required to sustain and enhance life. Of course, wealth must be produced before it can be consumed. This fact is the biggest flaw in the Aristocracy's agenda.

The Aristocracy acts as if wealth were a fact of nature, not the product of intelligence and hard work. Of course, wealth is not a fact of nature. The confiscation of the producer's wealth and Bureaucratic action inhibiting production will reduce the production of wealth.

A general reduction on the standard of living will certainly be the result of the Aristocracy's agenda.

THE POLITICAL SPECTRUM

Conventional wisdom has Communism and Socialism on the extreme left of the political spectrum, and Fascism on the extreme right. This would put Capitalism and the Mixed Economy in the center. Actually, the only difference between Socialism, Communism and Fascism and other forms of tyranny is the title of the Dictator, all three are just nomenclature for tyranny. This fallacy was perpetuated by Hitler and Mussolini during their campaign for power. Both portrayed Fascism as extreme right wing alternative to, and enemy of both Socialism and Communism, just political rhetoric. The name of the NAZI Party was "National Socialist German Workers' Party." For the political spectrum to make any sense, all tyranny must be located on the extreme left. The real political spectrum is Tyranny (Communism, Socialism, Fascism, etc.) on the extreme left, the Mixed Economy in the center and Capitalism (individual liberty) on the extreme right.

THE ARISTOCRACY'S PLAN

When the Aristocracy took control of Congress in 2006, the economy began to falter and their accumulation of power & wealth accelerated.

In 2008 Aristocracy won the Presidency. Their plan took off like a rocket and the Aristocracy completed its initiative to gain total control over the puppet press. The economy continued its deep decline and it was "all George Bush's fault." Of course, when the Puppet Press chose to report a good, growing economy, it was the "President's achievement." Just a reminder, the truth is irrelevant to both the Aristocracy and the Puppet Press.

Remember, both Hitler and Mussolini came to power as a result of economic crisis. Of course the objective of the Aristocracy is a Dictatorship. An economic crisis is required to replace a Republic with a Dictatorship!

DECLARING A DICTATORSHIP

On February 24, 2011 President Obama declared himself a Dictator when he informed Congress that he would ignore the real laws that he is sworn to uphold. He creates new laws with executive orders and Bureaucratic regulations.

Mr. Obama is not dumb, stupid or simply misguided as many people seem to think. He is flawlessly executing a plan to create a nation of slaves by reinstating the tyranny of King George III. But under new management!

The Aristocracy's priorities:
- **Consolidate their power**
- **Neutralize the opposition**
- **Disarm the citizens**

A DICTATORSHIP IS DECLARED
THE CONSTITUTION IS QUASHED

EXECUTIVE ORDERS ARE THE "LAW OF THE LAND"

ONLY SELECTED LAWS WILL BE ENFORCED.

THIS CAN ONLY BE DESCRIBED AS SLAVERY

DUTIES OF THE PRESIDENT LISTED IN
UNITED STATES CONSTITUTION.
ARTICLE. II,SECTION.3.
"he shall take Care that the Laws be faithfully executed"

LEGISLATIVE POWERS
THE UNITED STATES CONSTITUTION
ARTICLE 1,SECTION 1
"All legislative powers granted shall be vested in the Congress of the United States, which shall consist of a Senate and House of Representatives."

Commonsense21c.com

HOW TO CREATE AN ECONOMIC CRISIS

Why should the Aristocracy want to create an economic crisis?   An economic crisis would justify declaration of martial law, suspending the Constitution and establishing a Dictatorship! Both Hitler & Mussolini seized power during economic crises.

The actions taken by the Aristocracy in the past few years leave little doubt that creating an economic crisis is the objective.

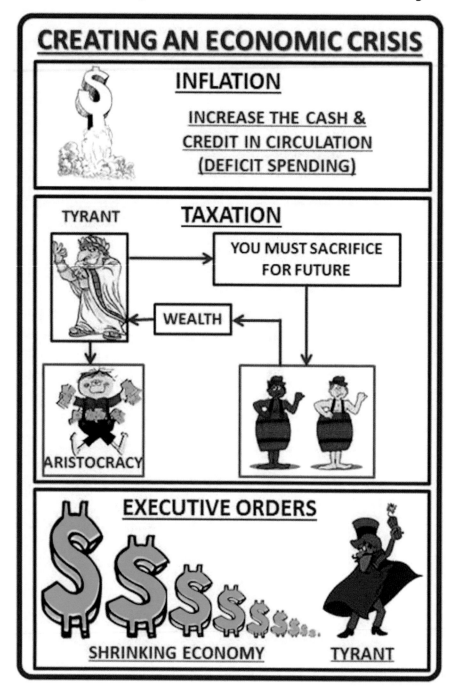

CHANGE YOU CAN BELIEVE IN!

"Change you can believe in" carried to its logical conclusion.

During the 2008 presidential campaign, Mr. Obama repeated the phrase "change you can believe in" many times. It is now 2013, and it is clear that the "change you can believe in" is converting us into the 21st Century serfs.

The Aristocracy has complete control of the Puppet Press. The Puppet Press is dispensing their propaganda, attacking their political enemies and ridiculing any opposition without regard for the truth.

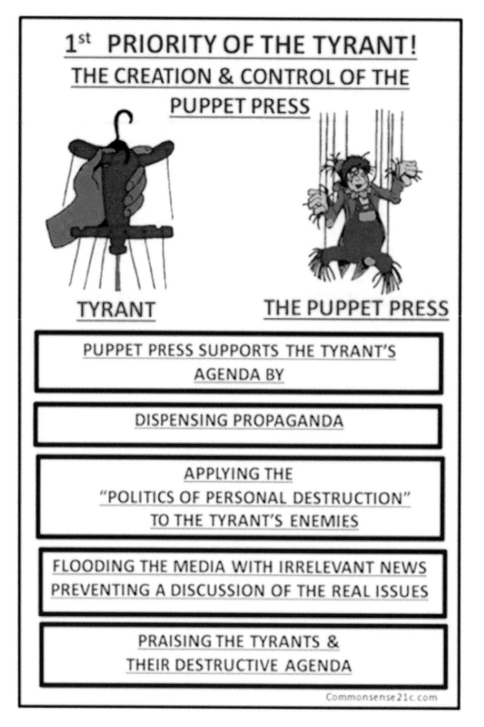

Are you dancing to the Aristocracy's music? The President's Press Secretary (conductor) and the Puppet Press (the musicians) orchestrate the Aristocracy's propaganda

The Puppet Press must, somehow, spin a logical and reasonable presentation of the Aristocracy's propaganda definitely not an easy job. Unable to spin the Aristocracy's agenda into a reasonable and believable press release, as a last resort, and in desperation, the Puppet Press turns to the 18th Century spinning wheel.

During the 2008 election campaign for President, "the race card" was an integral part of the Puppet Press program. The Puppet Press implied, but did not actually state, that it would be racist to vote for a white person. Once the election was completed and the new President took office, the Puppet Press was filled with statements from celebrities, stating that it was "racist to oppose the President's Agenda". Nowhere in the Puppet Press was there a hint that there could be a legitimate reason for opposing the President's Agenda. It did not take a genius to know that ill-conceived deficit spending was destroying the economy. How can it be racist to oppose an ill-conceived agenda that will create an economic crisis?

The years have shown that the President's Agenda has been a disaster and it continues to destroy the economy and weaken our nation!

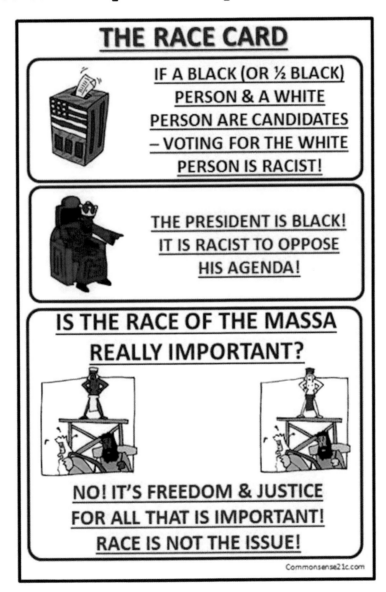

BIPARTISAN POLITICS ACCLAIMED BY THE PUPPET PRESS.

Many successful Republican politicians are RINOS (Republicans in name only). Often, controversial legislation requires the endorsement of the opposition party to scam a skeptical public. The Aristocracy praises the opposition as "bipartisan" and bribes the RINOS with support for their pet legislation to pass such controversial legislation. During the last 2 elections, the Aristocracy's strategy was to control both candidates. RINOS & Democrats are interchangeable.

NO MORE STINKING LAWS.

A tactic of the Aristocracy is to pass ambiguous and vague laws which allow an aggressive prosecutor make anyone a criminal. Those selected for prosecution are generally a threat to the ruling Aristocracy. An example of the vague, ambiguous laws is the 2000+ page legislation that created Obamacare. A Nation of criminals is extremely easy for the Aristocracy to control.

THE ARISTOCRACY'S POLITICAL CAMPAIGNS

Are the Aristocracy's campaign speeches real promises or just campaign rhetoric? First, you must remember that the Aristocracy's only requirement is that the statement enhances their goals. The truth is irrelevant and the Aristocracy is always in campaign mode.

Aristocracy's candidate was a charismatic speaker. The speeches were filled with great phrases like "change you can believe in." These phrases actually have no meaning and allow the audience to believe whatever it wants. But occasionally the speeches contained actual promises with defined meanings. Are these real and valid promises and information or just campaign rhetoric? Here is a short list of those statements, you decide on the validity.

- Eliminate deficit spending.

- Stimulus plan will reduce the unemployment rate to 5.4%.

- Obama care will lower health care premiums by $2500 per year per family.

- "If you like your health care plan, you'll be able to keep your health care plan, period."

- The Afghan war will be completed in June 2011.

- We reject sweeping claims of inherent presidential power. (2008)

- Executive actions: "we will not use signing statements, to nullify undermined duly enacted laws". (2008) (executive orders?)

- "My administration is committed to creating an unprecedented level of openness in the government, we will work together to ensure the public trust and establish a system of transparency, public participation, and collaboration. Open this will strengthen our democracy and promote efficiency and effectiveness in government." (June 2009)

The above list is a very small portion of the misinformation perpetuated by the Aristocracy over the past few years. However, it is more than sufficient to destroy the Aristocracy's credibility. The Aristocracy's information is totally worthless when trying to determine their future actions.

CAN A TELEPROMPTER ACTUALLY BE DANGEROUS?

For his speeches, Mr. Obama relies heavily upon his Teleprompter, apparently reading that Teleprompter verbatim. If the Teleprompter malfunctioned and flashed the truth, would the President choke on that truth?

TRANSPARENCY IN GOVERNMENT

During the 2008 campaign, the Aristocracy promised to increase transparency in government. In fact, they promised total transparency. Then they had a problem passing the Obamacare law. The Obamacare law was over 2000 pages long, that's about 1 &1/3 times the length of the Bible. Could anyone actually read over 2000 pages of such a boring document? The size of the document alone was adequate to hide its content.

Most of the Congress was not allowed to have a copy of the Obamacare law before it was passed through Congress and signed into law by the President. Few had any idea of its content, because its content was not released to most of Congress, and certainly not the public before it became law. Ms. Pelosi, the Speaker of the House, stated, "We have to pass it quickly so we can find out what's in it." Could she be a relative of Alfred E Newman?

Is this the Aristocracy's idea of transparency in the government?

RESULTS PROVE
THE OBAMA PRESIDENTIAL CAMPAIGN
WAS JUST "CAMPAIGN RHETORIC"

DECLINING ECONOMY

TRANSPARENCY IN GOVERNMENT
ENACTING OBAMACARE INTO LAW WHILE WITHHOLDING THE CONTENT FROM BOTH CONGRESS AND THE PEOPLE!

MS. PELOSI:
"WE HAVE TO PASS IT QUICKLY SO THAT WE CAN FIND OUT WHAT'S IN IT."

Commonsense21c.com

THE PELOSI LEGACY

Ms. Pelosi, then speaker of the house, pushed the Obamacare legislation through the Congress, while maintaining the content of the legislation secret. Should a congressional vote be valid when Congress persons don't know the content of the proposed legislation? A Constitutional Amendment requiring that Congresspersons pass a quiz on the content of legislation before they can vote is now a necessity. This is certainly a problem the Founding Fathers never foresaw!

The Pelosi legacy must be eliminated before it destroys the Republic!

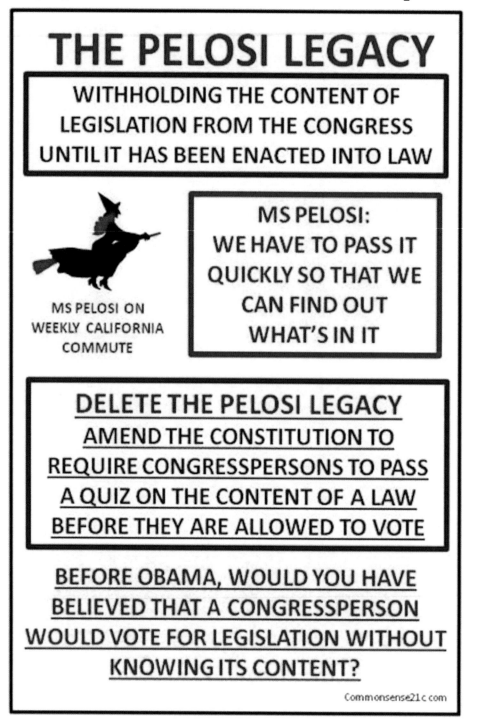

Did you ever wonder why the Bureaucracy is so effective in the Aristocracy's battle against the patriot? The Bureaucracy creates new rules daily and when the Bureaucracy finds that you have violated those rules you are guilty until proven innocent in a court of law.

Few people have the resources to challenge the Bureaucracy in court so in most cases the Bureaucracy's ruling stands without challenge.

Even if you are completely innocent and very wealthy, the fight to clear your name would be devastating.

THE AWESOME POWERS OF THE BUREAUCRACY

The Bureaucracy has total discretion in selecting its victims. Generally, the victims are passed to the Bureaucracy by powerful politicians. The politicians of course have their own agenda and expect to enhance their power and wealth through the action of the Bureaucracy.

Our Constitution guarantees that our citizens are innocent until proven guilty. This constitutional right is violated when a citizen is sanctioned by the Bureaucracy. When the Bureaucracy acts, the sanctions are applied and the victim is guilty until proven innocent in a court of law.

The awesome power of the Bureaucracy is ideally suited to eliminate those who pose a threat to the Aristocracy.

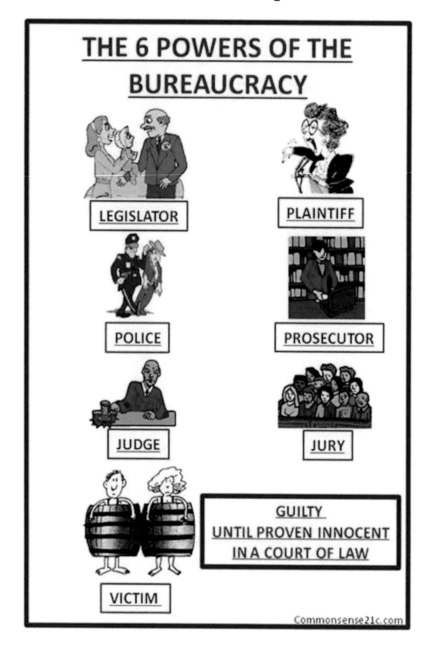

An invention that reduces the cost of providing a product or service improves the standard of living for all who consume the fruits of that invention. Occasionally an invention is conceived that provides an entirely new function, a function that had been unavailable to the public. The advantages of a new invention or technology are sometimes called the "Technology Dividend." The "Technology Dividend" is a mitigating factor in the continual inflation of currency. However, it can have a devastating effect on a prosperous industry as it renders that industry's production facilities and technology worthless. The Technology Dividend can destroy an existing industry, even as it enhances the standard of living for all.

Often, the owners of the endangered industry try to use political pressure to prevent the new product or technology from being marketed. Their weapon of choice, of course, is the Bureaucracy. The Technology Dividend in a Capitalist Society could provide economic growth as high a 10% per year.

"21st CENTURY COMMON SENSE" provides considerable information on the value of the "Technology Dividend" to our economy.

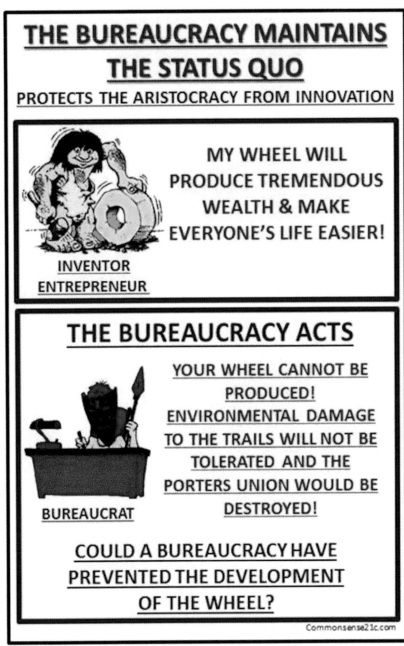

THE ARISTOCRACY SELECTS THE VICTIM!

The ruling Aristocracy has considerable competition. There are those who like the Cronyism Economy but want the wealth & power for themselves. There are those, like the Heroes of Ayn Rand's books (the modern Prometheus), whose motivation is achievement and the creation of wealth.

Even the capacity of the Bureaucracy is limited. The Aristocracy must select victims who are the greatest threat. If you get on their list, may God have mercy on your soul! The Bureaucracy has no conscience, only the desire to increase its budget. For the Bureaucracy to increase its budget, it is necessary to perpetuate and expand the Aristocracy.

When the Bureaucracy selects you as a victim, you are presumed guilty. If the Bureaucracy is unable to find a violation, they can create rules that you cannot avoid violating. To understand the motivation of the Bureaucracy, read the pamphlet, "Toby's Fable, "a Kindle document available from Amazon.com in December, 2013

THE ARISTOCRACY USES GOVERNMENT FORCE TO PUNISH POLITICAL DISSENT

The Republic cannot exist when the Aristocracy is free to use government force against their political enemies. No free society can survive when political action is punished by a Bureaucracy with the power to hold its victim guilty until proven innocent. This action by the Aristocracy is the greatest danger to our Republic.

Unfortunately, this is not a new problem. Both FDR and Nixon used the IRS to punish their political enemies and enhance their reelection chances. "21st CENTURY COMMON SENSE" has more information on this abuse and its bibliography has links to the website use for researching the book. It is illegal for the Aristocracy to target political enemies for prosecution because of their political activity. Since Aristocracy controls the Justice Department, do you actually expect them to prosecute themselves for this activity?

It took an Independent Special Prosecutor to bring down President Nixon for his illegal activities. One of the charges against Mr. Nixon was the use of the IRS to target and prosecute his political enemies. If we are to

protect ourselves from the Aristocracy's vendetta, a permanent Independent Special Prosecutor is necessary.

A vindictive investigation and prosecution by the IRS is a devastating and potentially bankrupting experience. Even if you're vindicated by the courts, your life and your ability to engage in political dissent can be destroyed.

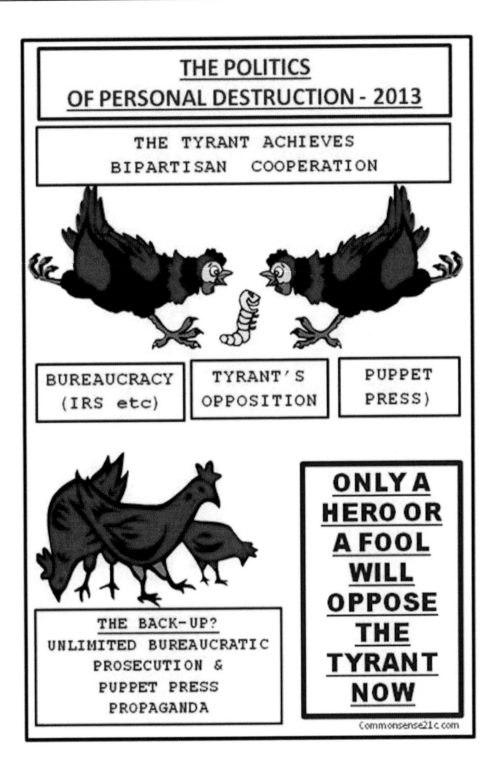

<u>PRESIDENT DENIES KNOWLEDGE OF THE IRS VENDETTA.</u>

The Aristocracy, through the Puppet Press, has denied that the President had any involvement in the IRS vendetta. Which is more dangerous to the Republic?

- An Aristocrat, using government resources to destroy his political enemies
- An incompetent clown, oblivious of the crimes being committed by his administration

The Republic cannot survive political persecution regardless of the source of that persecution.

INFLATION IS STEALTH TAXATION.

The debate over taxes is irrelevant! Taxes are levied when the government spends money. Tax laws only decide who pays. If the taxes don't cover government expenditures the result is inflation. Inflation is a tax on the value of money (inflation) and by definition, every dollar you own will buy less goods and services. When the Aristocracy promises no new taxes and votes for deficit spending, it is simply another self-serving lie.

Inflation is a contributing factor to the Aristocracy's goal of creating an economic crisis.

<u>THE GREAT GLOBAL WARMING SCAM.</u>
THE GREAT GLOBAL WARMING SCAM! Never in the field of human endeavor
have so many worked so hard to expand poverty throughout the land.
**The cost of energy is a big part of everyone's budget. The Great
Global Warming Scam is the Aristocracy's attempt to increase your
energy cost and allocate that increased cost to themselves and their
cronies.**

The Great Global Warming Scam is perpetuated by the Aristocracy to justify increasing taxes and government control over the individual. If you think that this cartoon is an exaggeration, remember, the EPA has classified hay a pollutant. That's right, hay, the stuff you feed to cattle. Don't take this cartoon literally. Cartoons, sometimes exaggerate to make a point. In this case, it would be difficult to exaggerate.

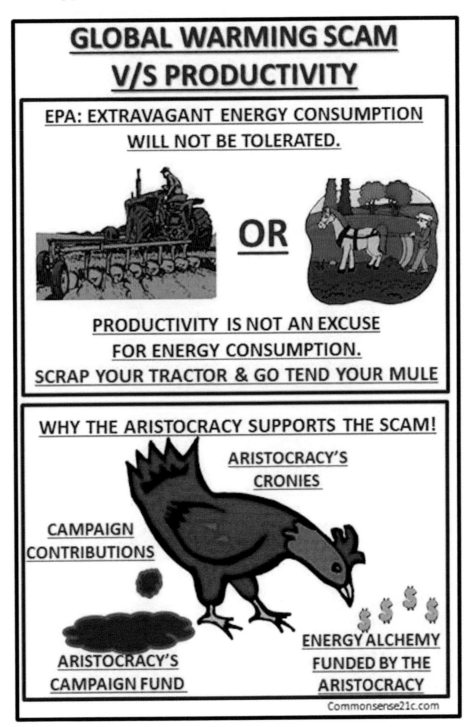

THE POLAR BEAR CUB ARGUMENT FOR THE GREAT GLOBAL WARMING
SCAM.

The Aristocracy, using the Puppet Press orchestrated a public-
relations blitz depicting a lovable little polar bear cub. It was
claimed that the global warming would eliminate the Arctic ice flows
that was the polar bear's habitat. No mention was made that a adult
polar bear was a predator that preyed on many other species and was
one of the only species left on earth that would stalk man.
Aristocracy will use any argument, no matter how flawed, to advance
the Great Global Warming Scam.
The claim that the polar bear was an endangered species was false.

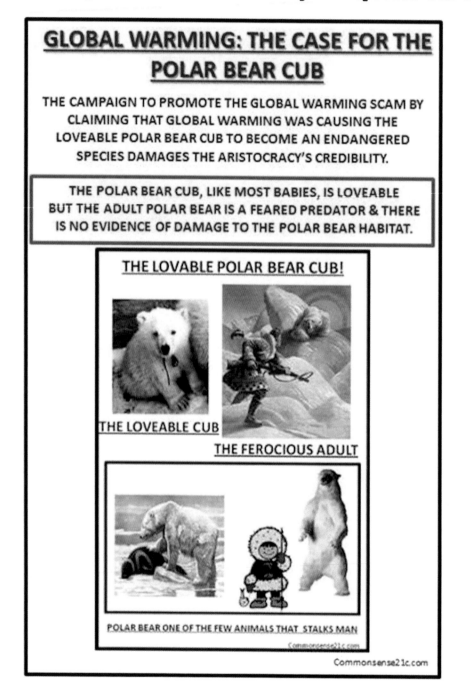

BLAME AND RECOVERY

When the recovery promised by the Aristocracy does not materialize (either by incompetency or on purpose) how does the Aristocracy escape the blame? The predecessor is blamed until the problem goes away. FDR blamed Hoover for 8 years.

DO EXECUTIVE ORDERS CREATE LEGAL LAWS?

Mr. Obama continues to create illegal laws by issuing Executive Orders. This action is in defiance of the promise he made during his first campaign for the Presidency and the oath he took to uphold the Constitution.

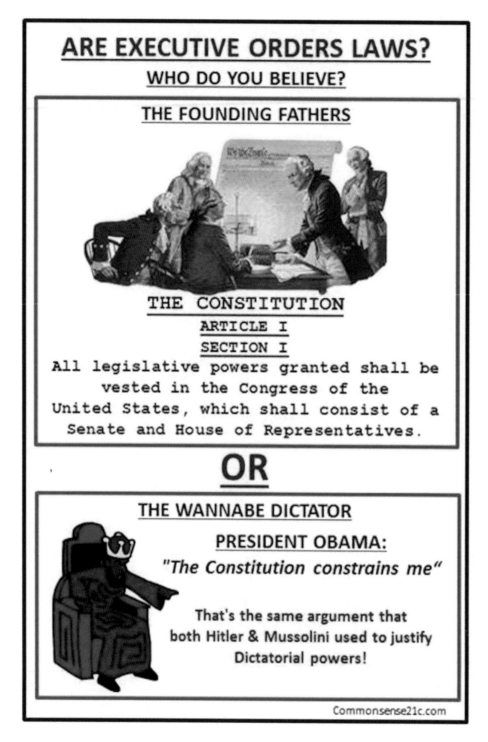

THE FINAL ACT-DISARMING THE PATRIOTS

Complete consolidation of the Aristocracy's power is achieved when Patriots are disarmed. Lexington Green, the shot heard around the world, occurred when King George III attempted to disarm the patriots and gain control of the Colonies. Will the Aristocracy succeed where the British failed in 1776?

The Aristocracy admits that it is constrained by the Constitution, but doesn't allow that fact to affect their actions!

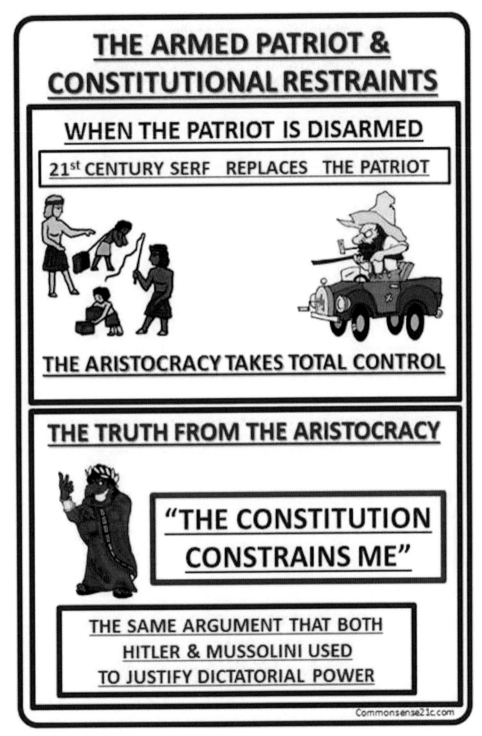

HOW CAN A BLOODY REVOLUTION BE AVOIDED?

The Aristocracy has ignored the Constitution that they swore to uphold when they took office. Illegal "Executive Orders" are being enforced and Aristocracy is using the Bureaucracy to punish political dissent on a "guilty until proven innocent" basis. Appointment of a "Special Independent Prosecutor" is our only chance, a very slight chance, to avoid a bloody revolution.

If a revolution occurs, the most likely conclusion will be a Dictatorship. Though, perhaps not the same Aristocracy that initiated the agenda that resulted in the Revolution.

The Aristocrats, executing an agenda that causes a revolution, should recall the fate of disposed tyrants. It is in everyone's best interest to avoid a bloody revolution because there is unlikely to be a real winner. There will, however be many losers.

BOOKS BY FELTON WILLIAMSON, JR.

"21st CENTURY COMMON SENSE"
Explains how we have allowed the Aristocracy to destroy our flawed capitalistic system and replace it with the tyranny of King George III, under new management. The disastrous results of the aristocracy's five s highly touted programs:

- The Income Tax Laws
- Inflation
- Antitrust Laws
- Earmarks
- The Bureaucracy

Included in the book are the economic advantages of the "Technology Dividend", the greatest threat to our Republic, and a recipe to regain our freedom and prosperity are included.

"COMMON SENSE THE WAY BACK"
An abridged version of "21st CENTURY COMMON SENSE"

"THE TEA PARTY & THE TYRANT"
A group of articles describing the conflict between the tea party and the Aristocracy

"TOBY'S FABLE"   (To be released in late December 2013)
A short fictional account of how the Bureaucracy abuses its victims, maintains the status quo, and increases everyone's cost of living.

Made in the USA
Charleston, SC
21 January 2014